yorkshire

D0615739

understanding and
caring for your breed

Written by
Michael James

yorkshire terrier

understanding and
caring for your breed

Written by
Michael James

Pet Book Publishing Company

The Old Hen House, St Martin's Farm, Zeals, Warminster, Wiltshire, BA12 6NZ

Printed and bound in South Korea

ISBN: 978-1-910488-21-8

Acknowledgements

The publishers would like to thank the following for help with photography: Wendy White Thomas (Wenwytes); Janet Redhead (Jankeri); Rita Harbury (Antara); Kay Morris (Wedgewood); Suzanne Robertsson (Doggy-Boons) and Amanda Bulbeck.

Contents

Introducing the Yorkie

A glamorous toy dog certainly but the Yorkshire Terrier is tough, He is the epitome of a big dog in a small package.

Characteristics

The key to understanding the Yorkshire Terrier is in his name. He is first and foremost a terrier, and has all the terrier characteristics. He is fearless and tenacious, and can have a surprisingly strong hunting instinct.

Always on the alert, he is full of curiosity and likes to be where the action is. He is small in size but he has a big heart and is loving and loyal with his family.

The Yorkshire Terrier has been bred down from larger terriers and is widely recognised as one of the most eye-catching of breeds in the show ring.

If his coat is allowed to grow to full length, it reaches

down to the floor and the beautiful combination of blue steel and rich tan colouring is truly stunning. The coat texture is a very special Yorkie characteristic; it is fine and silky and is more akin to human hair than conventional dog hair.

Keeping a Yorkshire Terrier in full coat is hugely demanding, so the majority of owners opt for a smart pet trim which is easy to maintain and allows the dog far greater freedom. For information on coat care, see page 102.

In terms of overall appearance, the Yorkie is a neat, well proportioned dog. He walks with his head held high, which gives an impression of confidence and self assurance.

He has a small head with v-shaped ears which are carried erect. His eyes speak volumes; they are dark and simply sparkle with intelligence – and mischief!

Traditionally, the Yorkshire Terrier had a docked tail, but this is outlawed in many countries, with the exception of the USA, and we are now used to seeing Yorkies with full tails.

Living with a Yorkie

The Yorkshire Terrier is supremely adaptable. He is small enough to be content in a tiny apartment, but he is perfectly happy to lord it in a big country house.

He will potter in a garden but will also be more than happy to go on hearty walks.

Below: *The Yorkie may be small but he has the heart of a lion.*

However, it is worth bearing in mind that some Yorkies bred from show lines are very small and if you are looking for a more robust companion, you need to go for a larger dog (see What Do You Want from Your Yorkie, page 32).

Family life can be hectic, but even though the Yorkshire Terrier is small he can stand up to the hustle and bustle.

Obviously children must be taught how to treat the family pet – he is definitely not a toy to be tugged and teased – but if mutual respect is established the Yorkie will be an outstanding companion and playmate.

It is worth bearing in mind that the Yorkshire Terrier has quite a strong prey drive which can be traced back to his roots as a formidable ratter.

Care must be taken if you have a cat in the family, or any other small animals. Harmonious co-

existence can be established but it should not be taken for granted. Time spent on supervising initial interactions will be well spent.

In terms of training, the Yorkshire Terrier is a highly intelligent dog and he relishes the opportunity to use his brain. A bored Yorkie may well become a destructive Yorkie – you have been warned!

Health and longevity

We are fortunate that the Yorkshire Terrier is a very healthy dog, and although he is prone to some breed specific disorders (see page 184) , he has a very good life expectancy.

The majority of Yorkies will reach their teens with some making it to their mid teens.

In a few, exceptional cases, Yorkies will do even better than this and there are records of dogs reaching their late teens.

Tracing back in time

Despite his name, the Yorkshire Terrier has his roots in Scotland, and even though he is universally recognised today as a toy dog, his ancestors were tough, working terriers.

It is thought that a number of breeds contributed to the make-up of the Yorkshire Terrier, and they were all valued as top-class rat catchers. The breeds include:

Skye Terrier: Taking its name from the Isle of Skye, this is one of Scotland's oldest Terrier breeds, and is still around today. Formerly used for vermin control, the Skye Terrier is now a valued companion and show dog.

The Clydesdale Terrier: No longer in existence, this breed was found around Glasgow and in the Clyde Valley. It bore a strong resemblance to the

Skye Terrier and had a bright steel, blue coat with tan markings, very similar to the Yorkshire Terrier's distinctive colouring.

Paisley Terrier: Very similar to the Clydesdale, the Paisley Terrier came from the Paisley area of Glasgow and was kept in the weaving sheds to keep down vermin. In appearance, he was a long, low dog with heavily fringed ears and a long, straight coat that was the texture of fine silk.

Black and Tan Terrier: This little dog was used for poaching rabbits. He would be sent down a rabbit hole to bolt the prey into a net that was spread over the exit. The dog and rabbits would then be put into the poacher's large pockets for a hasty retreat. It is thought that the Black and Tan was later bred with the dainty, long-coated Maltese which resulted in smaller, more refined offspring.

Creating the Yorkshire Terrier

During the industrial revolution of the 19th century, workers from Scotland migrated to Yorkshire to work in the weaving mills. They brought their families with them and were accompanied by their pet dogs who doubled up as rat catchers. In their new home in the north of England, there was plenty of work for the Scottish bred terriers, keeping down

vermin in the mills and weaving sheds. Over a period of time, these working terriers interbred producing a dog that became known as the Scotch or Broken-haired Terrier, and this is the direct ancestor of today's Yorkshire Terrier.

The Yorkie may be classed as a toy dog, but he is a true terrier at heart...

Developing the breed

By the 1850s dogs were being exhibited at shows - which were mainly held in public houses. Initially classed as a Scotch Terrier, it was not until the 1870s that the Yorkshire Terrier gained recognition in his own right.

Father of the breed

There is one single dog – Huddersfield Ben – who had an outstanding influence on the breed, and it can be claimed that every Yorkshire Terrier today relates back to his bloodlines.

Born in 1865, he was a fairly large dog and was shown in classes for dogs over 7lb (3.2kg) but under 12lb (5.2 kg). Bred by Mr Westwood, he was shown by Mrs Jonas Foster, the wife of a mill owner, who was an ardent pioneer of the new breed.

Huddersfield Ben died at the age of six but he was

used extensively at stud and had a massive impact on the development of the breed.

American Fame

Not long after the Yorkshire Terrier received official recognition in the UK in 1874, American breeders took an interest and organised imports of the new breed. The first Yorkies to be registered were Butch, born in 1882 and Daisy, born two years later. However, it was the breed's first American Champion, Bradford Harry, that established the breed in its new home.

Huddersfield Ben: Founder of the breed.

Bradford Harry was born in 1885 and was a direct descendant of the famous Huddersfield Ben. He was a successful show dog and was made up to be a Champion in 1889. But his significance was as a sire; he produced top quality offspring and put his stamp on the development of the breed in the USA.

The Modern Era

The dual charms of the Yorkshire Terrier – his loving, mischievous temperament combined with his stunning good looks – has ensured worldwide popularity. He is a brilliant companion dog, adapts to a variety of lifestyles and remains one of the most spectacular show dogs. To produce a top quality Yorkshire Terrier and present it in full coat is one of the greatest challenges in the show world. Over the years there have been many dedicated breeders, and the Yorkshire Terrier has earned all the top honours.

One of the greatest dogs of the modern era must be Ch. Ozmillion Mystification, the only Yorkshire Terrier to win Best in Show at Crufts. Bred by Osman Sameja of the famous Ozmillion Kennels, Mystification won 50 Challenge Certificates, 48 Best of Breeds, 22 Toy Groups, nine Best in Show club shows and three Best in Show All Breed Championship shows, including Crufts in 1997 – a truly outstanding record which will probably never be equalled.

What should a Yorkshire Terrier look like?

A Yorkshire Terrier in full sail, moving across the show ring with his coat streaming out, is a sight to behold. But there is more to a dog than his coat, so what should the perfect Yorkie look like?

If you speak to most owners of Yorkshire Terriers they will tell you they have the perfect dog and, of course, they do.

Pet owners are not looking for perfection as in the world of show dogs; they are looking for the dog that is perfect for what they want. As long as he is obedient, has a good temperament and is easy to live with, he is perfect in their eyes.

In the world of show dogs, the perfect dog does not and will never exist; every dog has his faults. All breeders can do is strive to produce a dog that is fit for function and adheres as closely as possible to the Breed Standard, which is the written blueprint describing what the breed should look like.

In the show ring, the judge does not compare dog against dog, but each dog against the Breed Standard. The dog that, in their opinion, comes nearest to the Standard, is the winner.

However the Breed Standard is open to interpretation and because of this you don't get the same dog winning all the time.

There are a number of governing bodies that authorise Breed Standards, most notably the Kennel Club in the UK, the American Kennel Club and the Federation Cynologique Internationale (FCI) which legislates for

89 member countries. There are minor difference between the UK and American Standards; the FCI takes its Standard from a breed's country of origin, and therefore follows the dictates of the UK Standard.

General appearance

The Yorkshire Terrier is a neat, compact dog with a well proportioned body. He has an upright carriage which gives him an air of importance. Show dogs have long, straight coats; the hair hangs down evenly on both sides with a parting that extends from the nose to the end of the tail.

Temperament

Alert and intelligent, the Yorkie is spirited but is also valued for his even disposition.

Head and skull

The head is small and rather flat on top; the skull should not rounded or too prominent which would be reminiscent of a Chihuahua. The muzzle should not be too long – about one-third of the skull depth is correct. The nose should be black.

Eyes

The eyes are medium-sized and are placed to look directly forward. They should be dark in colour with a sparkling expression that conveys intelligence. The eye rims should be dark.

Ears

The head has a look of elegance so the ears must be small and neat. They are v-shaped and carried erect. The ears are the only part of a Yorkie that are shorthaired; the colour should be a deep, rich tan.

Mouth

The teeth should meet in a scissor bite with the teeth on the upper jaw closely overlapping the teeth on the lower jaw.

Neck

The head is carried proudly and for this a Yorkie needs a good reach of neck. In practical terms, this means that if you put your hand on the neck you should be able to get three or four fingers between the back of the ears and the shoulders.

Forequarters

The shoulders are well laid; the legs are straight and they should be well covered with rich golden tan which should be a few shades lighter at the ends than at the roots.

The striking contrast of the rich tan head-fall and the steel blue body coat is a feature of the breed.

Body

The body is compact and there should be a good spring of rib as befits an active little dog. The back is level, and the loin (between the end of the ribcage and the start of the hips) is well defined.

Hindquarters

The hind legs are straight when viewed from behind, and there is a moderate turn of stifle (knee). The legs are well covered with rich, tan hair. Again, this is a few shades lighter at the ends, than at the roots.

Feet

These are round, and the nails should be black.

Tail

This is now undocked in the UK and most other countries, excluding the USA where it is docked to medium length.

In both cases, the tail is carried a little higher than the level of the back and should be as straight as possible so that the Yorkie looks balanced when on the move.

It is well covered with blue hair, which should be darker than the rest of the body.

Movement

The Yorkshire Terrier should move freely showing plenty of drive, and his top-line should remain level.

Coat and colour

The coat is the outstanding feature of the breed and the Breed Standard gives a detailed description of what is required in terms of type, texture ar d colour:

- The hair must be perfectly straight with no hint of a wave; it should be glossy and fine with the texture of silk.

- The hair on the body should be floor lencth in mature adults.

- The fall on the head is long and is traditionally tied in a topknot with a single bow. It is a rich golden tan, deeper in colour at the sides of the head.

- The hair on the muzzle is very long, and should also be a deeper tan.

- The tan on the head should not extend on to the neck, and there should be no intermingling of dark or sooty hair.

- The hair on the chest is a rich, bright tan, darker at the roots than in the middle, shading to still lighter at the tips.

- The hair on the body is a dark steel blue; it is important this has sufficient depth of colour so it is not silver blue. There must be no intermingling of fawn, bronze or dark hairs.

Size

The Yorkshire Terrier's size is assessed by weight – both dogs and bitches should not exceed 3.2kg (7lb)

Summing up

The majority of Yorkshire Terriers are kept as pet dogs and will never grow a full coat, let alone be exhibited in the show ring.

However, it is important that breeders strive for perfection and try to produce dogs that adhere as closely as possible to the Breed Standard. The top priority is to breed dogs that are both typical of the breed and sound in mind and body.

What do you want from your Yorkie?

There are hundreds of pedigree dog breeds to choose from so how can you be sure that the Yorkshire Terrier is the right dog for you? Before you decide on a Yorkie, you need to be 100 per cent confident that this is the breed that is best suited to your lifestyle.

Companion

The Yorkshire Terrier loves people – and he simply adores his family. If you want a loving and devoted companion, look no further. As an added bonus, the Yorkie is hugely entertaining as he takes an interest in everything that is going on.

He is the ideal pet for older people as he is not

demanding in terms of exercise, but his need for mental stimulation should not be neglected.

A Yorkie will make an excellent playmate for older children but he may not be the best choice if you have a very young family. This is a small dog, and although he thinks he is at least as big as a Rottweiler, he is not the most robust in physical terms. This applies particularly to Yorkies at the lower end of the size spectrum.

Watch dog

The Yorkie is keen and alert, and although he is not likely to see off intruders, he will certainly tell you when strangers are approaching. A Yorkie takes a pride in protecting his home, and although you want to keep yapping to a minimum a few warning barks can be very useful.

Sports dog

Quick thinking and intelligent, the Yorkshire Terrier has the brains to compete in all canine disciplines, but size is obviously a consideration. However, if you have a slightly bigger Yorkie – and you make your training rewarding and motivational, who knows what you can achieve. For more information, see Opportunities for Yorkies page 152.

Show dog

The Yorkshire Terrier is one of the most glamorous of all show dogs, and if you have the time and patience to learn the art of grooming and presentation, you will find the show ring a challenging and rewarding experience. Bear in mind that keeping a Yorkie in full coat is a massive undertaking and it does impact on a dog's lifestyle. Weigh up the pros and cons, and seek as much advice as possible, before taking this route. Showing can enrich your life – and your dog's life – but it is not for the faint-hearted.

For more information on showing, see page 158.

What does your Yorkie want from you?

A dog cannot speak for himself, so we need to view the world from a canine perspective and work out what a Yorkshire Terrier needs in order to live a happy, contented and fulfilling life.

Time and commitment

First of all, a Yorkie needs a commitment that you will care for him for the duration of his life – guiding him through his puppyhood, enjoying his adulthood, and being there for him in his later years.

If all potential owners were prepared to make this pledge, there would be scarcely any dogs in rescue. The Yorkie is a home-orientated dog; he loves his own special people and his greatest wish is to be included in family outings.

If he is excluded, or if he is expected to spend long periods on his own, he will be thoroughly miserable. He may pine, or he may become destructive, or get into the habit of barking continuously when he is left alone. If you have to be away from home for more than four hours at a stretch, delay dog ownership until your circumstances change. For advice on separation anxiety, see page 122.

Practical matters

The long-coated Yorkshire Terrier is a high maintenance breed in terms of coat care. If you opt for a pet trim – a sensible option for most owners – you need to budget for regular trips to the groomer, as well as providing routine care. If you plan to get involved in showing, your life will revolve around keeping your Yorkie in full coat, so a passion for grooming should be considered essential. For information on coat care, see page 102.

As already highlighted, the Yorkie is adaptable in terms of his exercise requirements. But he will certainly enjoy the stimulation of going to new places.

Training and leadership

You may think that a dog that is as small as a Yorkshire Terrier does not need much training, but this would be a big mistake. Regardless of size, the Yorkie is a 'proper' dog and should be treated as such. In fact, his terrier background means that he is more feisty than most toy breeds, and he is ready to take advantage if the occasion presents itself.

From an early age, a Yorkie needs to be trained and socialised so that he finds his place in the family pack and has no need to challenge it. In common with larger breeds, he needs to know where his boundaries lie, accepting and respecting your role as decision-maker.

If this side of his education is neglected, a Yorkie may try to call the shots. He may become possessive and guard his place on the sofa, refuse to give up a favourite toy, or resent interference when he is eating his food.

There are steps you can take to resolve these scenarios (see page 149) but it is far better to prevent them happening in the first place. Training and, most particularly, consistency is the key to success. Yorkshire Terriers are clever dogs, and mental stimulation should be considered a must.

This could take the form of training, which could be as ambitious as competing in a sport, more relaxed trick training, or something as simple as going out to lots of different places.

It does not matter what you do, but you need to bear in mind that a bored Yorkie will develop his own agenda, which could mean incessant barking plus other forms of attention-seeking which can become very challenging.

A Yorkie needs an owner he can love and respect.

Extra considerations

Now you have decided that a Yorkshire Terrier is the dog of your dreams, you can narrow your choice so you know exactly what you are looking for.

Male or female?

Whether you get a male or female Yorkie comes down to personal preference. There may be minor differences in temperament – some say females are quieter and calmer compared to males, which can be a little headstrong. However, all Yorkies are individuals, and character will depend more on bloodlines and rearing than on gender.

If you decide on a female, you will need to cope with her seasons, which will start at any time from six months onwards and occur either twice-yearly or every nine months thereafter. During the three-week period of a season, you will need to keep your bitch away from entire males (males that have not

been neutered) to eliminate the risk of an unwanted pregnancy. Some owners also report that females may be a little moody and withdrawn during their seasonal cycle. Many pet owners opt for neutering, which puts an end to the seasons, and also has many attendant health benefits. The operation, known as spaying, is usually carried out at some point after the first season. The best plan is to seek advice from your vet.

An entire male may not cause many problems, although some do have a stronger tendency to mark, which could include in the house. However, training will usually put a stop to this. An entire male will also be on the lookout for bitches in season, and this may lead to difficulties, depending on your circumstances. Neutering (castrating) a male is a relatively simple operation, and there are associated health benefits. Again, you should seek advice from your vet.

More than one?

Yorkies are highly collectible, and you may well decide you want to increase your dog population, or even build up a mini tribe of Yorkshire Terriers. Fortunately, Yorkies are sociable dogs and seem to enjoy each other's company. It certainly helps with issues of separation anxiety if you have more than one. Yorkshire Terriers are entirely fearless and will mix well with other breeds, regardless of their size. You may think a big dog will be the boss, but you can guarantee that it will be the Yorkie that rules the roost!

If you decide you want two Yorkies, do not make the mistake of getting two pups from the same litter, or even two youngsters who are close in age. The pups will have a great time, but they will bond with each other rather than with you. House training will be a nightmare, and unless you are truly dedicated and are prepared to allocate individual time for each dog, training will be a disaster.

If you do decide to take on a second Yorkshire Terrier wait at least 18 months so your first dog is fully trained and settled before embarking on a puppy. Same sex pairs and mixed pairs seem to get on equally well, but if you opt for a mixed pair, you will need to get one or both dogs neutered.

An older dog

You may decide to miss out on the puppy phase and take on an older dog instead. Such a dog may be harder to track down, but sometimes a breeder will rehome a female when her breeding career is at an end so she can enjoy the benefits of getting more individual attention. In some cases, the breeder may have run on a puppy as potential breeding stock and then found he/she is not suitable for this role, but will still make an excellent pet dog.

There are advantages to taking on an older dog, as you know exactly what you are getting. But the upheaval of changing homes can be quite upsetting, so you will need to have plenty of patience during the settling in period.

Rehoming a rescued dog

The Yorkshire Terrier is a popular breed and although they are easy to live with, it is inevitable that some adults find themselves in rescue. You may find a Yorkie in an all-breed rescue shelter, but breed clubs also run their own rescue schemes, and this may be a better option.

It is important to bear in mind that often a dog needs to be rehomed through no fault of his own, mostly when a family's circumstances change. The reasons are various, ranging from illness or death of the original owner to family breakdown, changing jobs, or even the arrival of a new baby. However, there are cases where a Yorkie has not received the training and socialisation he needs, and he may have behavioural issues, which need to be resolved. For this reason, think long and hard before you take on a rescue dog.

You need to be realistic about what you are capable of achieving so you can be sure you can give the dog in question a permanent home.

Regardless of the dog's previous history, you will need to give him plenty of time and be patient with him as he settles into his new home. It may take weeks, or even months before he becomes fully integrated in the family, but if all goes well you will have the reward of knowing that you have given a Yorkie a second chance.

Below: Try to discover a dog's background before making the decision to adopt.

Sourcing a puppy

Your aim is to find a healthy Yorkshire Terrier puppy that has been reared with the greatest possible care. Where do you start?

A tried-and-trusted method of finding a puppy is to attend a dog show where your chosen breed is being exhibited.

This will give you the opportunity to see lots of different Yorkies. The classes are divided between males and females and are age related so you will see puppies from as young as six months, veterans, and everything in between.

You will see differences in coat, as it takes at least two years for a dog to grow a full- length coat. But if you look closely, you will also see there are different 'types' on show.

They are all purebred Yorkshire Terriers, but breeders produce dogs with a family likeness, so you can see which type you prefer. When judging has been completed, talk to the exhibitors and find out more about their dogs. They may not have puppies available, but some will be planning a litter, and you may decide to put your name on a waiting list.

Internet research

The Internet is an excellent resource, but when it comes to finding a puppy, use it with care:

DO go to the website of your national Kennel Club.

Both the American Kennel Club (AKC) and the Kennel Club (KC) have excellent websites, which will give you information about the Yorkshire Terrier as a breed, and what to look for when choosing a puppy. You will also find contact details for specialist breed clubs.

Both sites have lists of puppies available, and you can look out for breeders of merit (AKC) and assured breeders (KC), which indicates that a code of conduct has been adhered to.

DO find details of specialist breed clubs.

On breed club websites you will find lots of useful information which will help you to care for your Yorkie. There may be contact details of breeders in your area, or you may need to go through the club secretary. Some websites also have a list of breeders that have puppies available. The advantage of going through a breed club is that members will follow a code of ethics, and this will give you some guarantees regarding breeding stock and health checks.

If you are planning to show your Yorkshire Terrier you will need to find a breeder that specialises in show lines, and has a reputation for producing top quality dogs.

Remember that health and temperament are top priorities, so do not overlook these considerations when you are researching pedigrees.

DO NOT look at puppies for sale.

There are legitimate Yorkshire Terrier breeders with their own websites, and they may, occasionally, advertise a litter, although in most cases reputable breeders have waiting lists for their puppies.

The danger comes from unscrupulous breeders that produce puppies purely for profit, with no thought for the health of the dogs they breed from and no care given to rearing the litter.

Photos of puppies are hard to resist, but never make a decision based purely on an advertisement.

You need to find out who the breeder is, and have the opportunity to visit their premises and inspect the litter before making a decision.

Questions, questions, questions

When you find a breeder with puppies available, you will have lots of questions to ask. These should include the following:

- Where have the puppies been reared? Hopefully, they will be in a home environment, which gives them the best possible start in life.

- How many are in the litter?

- What is the split of males and females?

- How many have already been spoken for? The breeder will probably be keeping a puppy to show or for breeding, and there may be others on a waiting list.

Below: You may have to go on a waiting list – but the wait will be worth it!

- Can I see the mother with her puppies?

- What age are the puppies?

- When will they be ready to go to their new homes?

Bear in mind puppies need to be with their mother and siblings until they are a minimum of eight weeks of age otherwise they miss out on vital learning and communication skills which will have a detrimental effect on them for the rest of their lives. In fact, most Yorkie breeders prefer to wait until puppies are around ten weeks old before they go to their new homes as by this age they are a little bigger and more able to cope with the trauma of leaving the litter and their familiar surroundings.

You should also be prepared to answer a number of searching questions so the breeder can check if you are suitable as a potential owner of one of their precious puppies.

You will be asked some or all of the following questions:

- What is your home set up?

- Do you have children/grandchildren?

- What are their ages?

- Is there somebody at home the majority of the time?

- What is your previous experience with dogs?

- Do you already have other dogs at home?

- Do you want to exhibit your Yorkshire Terrier in the show ring?

- Do you have plans to compete with your Yorkie in one of the canine sports?

The breeder is not being intrusive; they need to understand the type of home you will be able to provide in order to make the right match. Do not be offended by this. The breeder is doing it for both the dog's benefit and also for yours.

Steer clear of a breeder who does not ask you questions. He or she may be more interested in making money out of the puppies, rather than ensuring that they go to good homes. They may also have taken other short cuts, which may prove disastrous, and very expensive, in terms of vet bills or plain heartache.

Puppy watching

A litter of Yorkshire puppies is totally irresistible. Rushing up to greet you, this band of mini ragamuffins – so different from the glamorous full-coated adults – all seem to say: "Take me home". However, you must try to put your feelings to one side so that you can make an informed choice.

You need to be 100 per cent confident that the breeding stock is healthy, and the puppies have been reared with love and care, before making a commitment to buy.

Viewing a litter

It is a good idea to have mental checklist of what to look out for when you visit a breeder. You want to see:

- A clean, hygienic environment.

- Puppies who are out-going, friendly, and eager to meet you.

- A sweet natured mother who is ready to show off her puppies.

- Pups that are well covered, but not pot-bellied (which could be an indication of worms).

- Bright eyes, with no sign of soreness or discharge.

- Clean ears that smell fresh.

- No discharge from the eyes or nose.

- Clean rear ends – matting could indicate upset tummies.

- Lively pups that are keen to play.

It is important that you see the mother with her

puppies, as this will give you a good idea of the temperament they are likely to inherit. It is also helpful if you can see other close relatives so you can assess the type and temperament that the breeder produces.

In most cases, you will not be able to see the father (sire) as most breeders will travel some distance to find a stud dog that is not too close to their own bloodlines and complements their bitch. However, you should be able to see photos of him and find out how he is bred, which will help you to make an informed decision.

Health issues

Like all purebred dogs, Yorkshire Terriers have a predisposition to some health disorders, which may or may not be inherited. Ask the breeder for a full history of the parents and preceding generations to see if there are any issues you need to be aware of. For more information, see Breed-specific disorders, page 182.

Companion puppy

In most cases, you will want a Yorkie purely and simply as a companion, and in this matter, your choice should be guided by the breeder. It is tempting to go for the pup that comes up to you first, or the one that makes you laugh as he chases his siblings.But the breeder will have spent hours and hours watching the puppies as they have developed from newborns.

He/she therefore has an in-depth knowledge of how the puppies interact with each other, with other dogs in the family, how they relate to people, and how they cope with new experiences. This is invaluable information when making the right match; the breeder will take into account your family set up and lifestyle and will help you to pick the most suitable puppy.

Show puppy

Do you have ambitions to exhibit your Yorkshire Terrier in the show ring?

If this is the case you need to make your intentions clear to the breeder so you can select a puppy that has the potential to be successful in the ring. The aim is to find a Yorkshire Terrier who will meet the stipulations set down in the Breed Standard.

This is no easy matter when a puppy is only eight to ten weeks old, but an expert can make an assessment, ensuring there are no obvious faults in conformation. Bear in mind that colour changes as a Yorkshire Terrier matures so a puppy that is black and tan should develop the steel blue and rich tan coat that is a hall mark of the breed. Temperament is of vital importance. Grooming is a lengthy business so you need a dog who is placid enough to cope with this on a daily basis, but also has the air of self importance and showmanship that will stand out in the ring.

A Yorkie friendly home

It may seem an age before your puppy is ready to leave the breeder and move to his new home. But you can fill the time by getting your home ready, and buying the equipment you will need. These preparations apply to a new puppy but, in reality, they are the means of creating an environment that is safe and secure for your Yorkie throughout his life.

In the home

Nothing is safe when a puppy is about, and despite his diminutive size, the Yorkie is no exception. Everything is new and exciting for a young puppy; it all needs thorough investigation – and this usually means testing with mouth and teeth.

One thing is certain – a free-ranging Yorkshire

Terrier puppy cannot be trusted! Remember, it is not only your prized possessions that are under threat; equally relevant is the damage a puppy can inflict on himself. Trailing electric cables are a major hazard so these will need to be secured out of reach. You will need to make sure all cupboards and storage units cannot be opened – or broken into. This applies particularly in the kitchen where you may store cleaning materials, and other substances, which could be toxic to dogs. There are a number of household plants that are poisonous, so these will need to be relocated, along with breakable ornaments.

It would be wise to declare upstairs off-limits as negotiating stairs can be hazardous for a tiny puppy. The best way of doing this is to use a baby gate – but make sure your puppy can't squeeze through it, or under it, when he is very small.

In the garden

It is unusual for a Yorkshire Terrier to stray far from his people but you need to check your garden is safe and secure. It has been know for a Yorkie to jump over a three foot (91cm) fence, so err on the side of caution and opt for fencing that is four feet (122 cm) in height. You also need to check that there are no gaps or holes he could squeeze through. If you have a gate leading out of the garden it should have a secure fastening, and you would be advised to put up a sign, reminding visitors to shut the gate.

Some Yorkies are enthusiastic gardeners, and will show no respect for your prized plants. This is bad news for you, but there is also a serious risk that your Yorkie could be in danger. There are a number of plants that are toxic to dogs so you need to check these out on the internet and remove them, or restrict access to them before your puppy comes home.

Swimming pools and ponds should be covered as most puppies are fearless and, although it is easy for a puppy to take the plunge, it is virtually impossible for him to get out unaided.

You will also need to designate a toileting area. This will assist the house-training process, and it will also make cleaning up easier. For information on house-training see page 90.

House rules

Before your puppy comes home, hold a family conference to decide on the house rules. You need to decide which rooms your puppy will have access to, and establish whether he is to be allowed on the furniture or not. The Yorkie sees himself as a lap dog

and a watch dog; his dual aims are to cuddle up with a member of his beloved family on the sofa, and to find a strategic observation point. Most owners take this on board, and the majority of Yorkies have free rein of the house.

However, your puppy needs to know where his boundaries lie otherwise he will push his luck and will not respect you as the decision-maker. When you have decided on the house rules, make sure you apply them consistently so your Yorkie understands what is required of him and is happy to co-operate.

Buying equipment

There are some essential items of equipment you will need for your Yorkshire Terrier. If you choose wisely, much of it will last for many years to come.

Indoor crate

Rearing a puppy is so much easier if you invest in an indoor crate. It provides a safe haven for your puppy at night, when you have to go out during the day, and at other times when you cannot supervise him. A puppy needs a base where he feels safe and secure, and where he can rest undisturbed. An indoor crate provides the perfect den, and many adults continue to use them throughout their lives. You will also need to consider where you are going to locate the crate.

The kitchen is usually the most suitable place as this is the hub of family life. Find a snug corner where the puppy can rest when he wants to, but where he can also see what is going on around him, and still be with the family.

Travel carrier

Your Yorkie's indoor crate can double up as a travel carrier, but it is easier to have accommodation that is kept in the car.

There are lots of different designs to choose from – from rigid, plastic carriers to canvas carriers. What you choose is a matter of personal preference, but check that the carrier has good ventilation so that your Yorkie does not get overheated.

Playpen

This is not essential but playpens are becoming increasingly popular with puppy owners. You can set up the playpen, line it with bedding and equip it with toys, and your puppy has a safe play space where he cannot find mischief.

Beds and bedding

The crate and travel carrier will need to be lined with bedding. The best type to buy is synthetic fleece, which is warm and cosy. It is also machine washable and easy to dry. An added advantage is that moisture soaks through the bedding, so when your puppy is going through the house training process there is no risk of him being left in a wet bed.

If you have purchased a crate, you may not feel the need to buy an extra bed. However, the Yorkie enjoys his creature comforts and he will certainly appreciate additional sleeping quarters. There is an amazing array of dog-beds to chose from – duvets, bean bags, cushions, baskets, igloos, mini-four posters – so you can take your pick! However, you do need to bear in mind that some beds prove irresistible as far as chewing is concerned, so delay making a major investment until your Yorkie has outgrown the destructive, puppy phase.

Collar and lead

You may think that it is not worth buying a collar for the first few weeks, but the sooner your pup gets used to it, the better (see Wearing a collar, page 134). A nylon lightweight collar is recommended, as most puppies will accept it without making a fuss. Be careful when you are fitting the collar that is not too tight, but equally not too loose; a good guideline is to make sure you can fit two of your fingers under the collar. You do not need a big, chunky lead for a Yorkie, but you need to ensure the lead you choose

*Always buy the best
quality equipment you
can afford.*

has a secure trigger fastening. Again, there are plenty to choose from, but make sure the lead is made of a material, such as leather or soft nylon, which will not chafe your hands.

An extending lead can be a useful purchase as you can give your Yorkshire Terrier limited freedom when it is not safe or permitted to allow him off lead. However, you should never use it when walking alongside roads as an unexpected pull from your Yorkie, resulting in the lead extending further than you intend, could have disastrous consequences.

ID

Your Yorkshire Terrier needs to wear some form of ID when he is out in public places. This can be in the form of a disc, engraved with your contact details, attached to the collar. When your Yorkie is full-grown, you can buy an embroidered collar with your contact details, which eliminates the danger of the disc becoming detached from the collar.

You may also wish to consider a permanent form of ID. Increasingly breeders are getting puppies micro-chipped before they go to their new homes.

A micro-chip is the size of a grain of rice. It is 'injected' under the skin, usually between the shoulder blades, with a special needle. It has some tiny barbs on it, which dig into the tissue around where it lies, so it does not migrate from that spot.

Each chip has its own unique identification number that can only be read by a special scanner.

That ID number is then registered on a national database with your name and details, so that if ever your dog is lost, he can be taken to any vet or rescue centre where he is scanned and then you are contacted.

If your puppy has not been micro-chipped, you can ask your vet to do it, maybe when he goes along for his vaccinations.

Bowls

Your Yorkie will need two bowls; one for food, and one for fresh drinking water, which should always be readily available.

A stainless steel bowl is a good choice for a food bowl. Plastic bowls will almost certainly be chewed, and there is a danger that bacteria can collect in the small cracks that may appear. You can opt for a second stainless steel bowl for drinking water, or you may prefer a heavier ceramic bowl, which will not be knocked over so easily.

Food

The breeder will let you know what your puppy is eating and should provide a full diet sheet to guide you through the first six months of your puppy's feeding regime – how much they are eating per meal, how many meals per day, when to increase the amounts given per meal and when to reduce the meals per day. The breeder may provide you with some food when you go and collect your puppy, but it is worth making enquiries in advance about the availability of the brand that is recommended.

Grooming gear

The equipment you need will depend on whether you are keeping your Yorkie in full coat or whether you plan to opt for a puppy trim. To get started you will need:

- Pure bristle brush: This should be a high quality brand which will go through the coat without damaging it.

- Steel comb: You will need a dual-purpose comb that has both coarse teeth and fine teeth.

- Nail-clippers: The guillotine type are easy to use.

- Toothbrush and toothpaste: Choose between a long-handled toothbrush or a finger brush, whichever you find easiest. There are flavoured

canine toothpastes on the market, which your dog will enjoy.

For information on grooming and keeping your Yorkshire Terrier in full coat, see pages 106-110.

Toys

Yorkshire Terriers love their toys – and this is not confined to puppies! The Yorkie's terrier side comes out when he is playing and he can be surprisingly rough and tenacious with his favourite toys. However, before you get carried away with buying a vast range of toys to keep your puppy entertained, you need to think about which are the safest. Plastic toys can be shredded, cuddly toys can be chewed, and toys where the squeaker can be removed should be avoided at all costs.

If your Yorkie ingests part of a toy, it could well result in an internal blockage, and the results of this are often fatal. Obviously the Yorkie is not as destructive as larger dogs, which gives you some leeway, but it is advisable to keep toys out of reach when your Yorkie is left on his own.

However, the only exception to this rule are the hard, rubber 'kong' toys, which can be stuffed with food. These are 100 per cent safe and will give your Yorkie an occupation when he needs to be left home alone.

Finding a vet

Before your puppy arrives home, you should register with a vet. Visit some of the vets in your local area, and speak to other pet owners, to find out who they recommend.

It is so important to find a good vet, almost as important as finding a good doctor for yourself. You need to find someone with whom you can build a good rapport and have complete faith in. Word of mouth is really the best recommendation. When you contact a veterinary practice, find out the following:

- Does the surgery run an appointment system?

- What are the arrangements for emergency, out-of-hours cover?

- What facilities are available at the practice?

- Do the vets in the practice have experience in treating Yorkshire Terriers?

If you are satisfied with what your find, and the staff appear to be helpful and friendly, book an appointment so your puppy can have a health check a couple of days after you collect him.

Settling in

When you first arrive home with your puppy, be careful not to overwhelm him. You and your family will be hugely excited, but the puppy is in a completely strange environment with new sounds, smells and sights. This is a daunting experience, even for the boldest of pups.

Some puppies are very confident, wanting to play straightaway and quickly making friends; others need a little longer. Keep a close check on your Yorkshire Terrier's body language and reactions so you can proceed at a pace he is comfortable with.

First, let him explore the garden. He will probably need to relieve himself after the journey home, so take him to the allocated toileting area and, when he performs, give him plenty of praise.

When you take your puppy indoors, let him investigate again. Show him his crate, and encourage him to enter by throwing in a treat. Let him sniff, and allow him to go in and out as he wants to.

Later on, when he is tired, you can put him in the crate while you stay in the room. In this way he will learns to settle and will not think he is being abandoned.

It is a good idea to feed your puppy in his crate, at least to begin with, as this helps to build up a positive association. It will not be long before your Yorkie sees his crate as his own special den and will go there as a matter of choice.

Some owners place a blanket over the crate, covering the back and sides, so that it is even more cosy and den-like.

Meeting the family

Resist the temptation of inviting friends and neighbours to come and meet the new arrival; your puppy needs to focus on getting to know his new family for the first few days. Try not to swamp your Yorkshire Terrier with too much attention – he needs a chance to explore and find his feet. There will be plenty of time for cuddles later on!

If you have children in the family, you need to keep everything as calm as possible. The Yorkie will make an outstanding family companion but a sense of mutual respect needs to be established. As already highlighted, a Yorkie is not the best choice for small children but older children also need to learn how to behave with the new addition to the family. The Yorkshire Terrier is small, but he is not a toy – and he is definitely not a baby! He needs to be treated like a proper dog, which means:

- He should not be constantly picked up and carried around.

- He should not be teased.

- He should be left in peace when he retires to his bed.

- He should not be disturbed when he is eating.

Bear in mind, it is easy for a puppy to become over-excited by raised voices, or by children running around and behaving unpredictably, and this can easily lead to mouthing and nipping.

The best plan is to get the children to sit on the floor and give them all a treat.

Each child can then call the puppy, stroke him, and offer a treat. In this way the puppy realizes that it is not a free for all, and that he needs to interact with each child calmly and sensibly in order to get his treat. If he tries to nip or mouth, make sure there is a toy at the ready, so his attention can be diverted to something he is allowed to bite. If you do this consistently, he will learn to inhibit his desire to mouth when he is interacting with people.

Right from the start, impose a rule that the children are not allowed to pick up or carry the puppy. They can cuddle him when they are sitting on the floor. This may sound a little severe, but a wriggly puppy can be dropped in an instant, sometimes with disastrous consequences.

Involve all family members with your puppy's day-to-day care; this will enable the bond to develop with the whole family as opposed to just one person. Encourage the children to train and reward the puppy, teaching him to follow their commands without question.

Spend time with your Yorkie and your children, teaching them to respect each other.

The animal family

Yorkies are generally sociable little dogs, and it is rare to have problems when introducing a new puppy to the resident animal family. However, it is best to take nothing for granted and to supervise early interactions.

In an ideal scenario, introduce your resident dog to the newcomer at the breeder's home. This works well as the puppy feels secure and the adult dog does not feel threatened. But if this is not possible, allow your dog to smell the puppy's bedding (the bedding supplied by the breeder is fine) before they actually meet so he familiarizes himself with the puppy's scent.

The garden is the best place for introducing the puppy, as the adult will regard it as neutral territory. He will probably take a great interest in the puppy and sniff him all over. Most puppies are naturally submissive in this situation, and your pup may lick the other dog's mouth or roll over on to his back. Try not to interfere as this is the natural way that dogs get to know each other.

You will only need to intervene if the older dog is too boisterous, and alarms the puppy. In this case, it is a good idea to put the adult on his lead so you have some measure of control.

It rarely takes long for an adult to accept a puppy, as he does not constitute a threat. This will be underlined if you make a big fuss of the older dog so that he has no reason to feel jealous.

Feline friends

Never forget that the Yorkie is a terrier at heart, and he may well take a lively interest in the family cat. However, harmonious relations can be established if you work hard at early interactions. You will need to progress step by step, making sure the pair are never left alone together until they have learnt to ignore each other.

If your Yorkie seems very focused on the cat, it may be easier to confine her in a carrier for the first couple of meetings, so your puppy has a chance to make her acquaintance in a controlled situation. Keep calling your puppy to you and rewarding him so that he does not get obsessed with cat watching. You can then graduate to holding your puppy while the cat is free, again rewarding him with a treat every time he responds to you and looks away from the cat. When you allow your puppy to go free, make sure the cat has an easy escape route, just in case he tries to chase.

This is an on-going process but all the time your Yorkie is learning that he is rewarded for ignoring the cat. In time, the novelty will wear off and the pair will live in peace – who knows, they may even become the best of friends!

Feeding

The breeder will generally provide enough food for the first few days so the puppy does not have to cope with a change in diet – and possible digestive upset – along with all the stress of moving home.

Some puppies eat up their food from the first meal onwards, others are more concerned by their new surroundings and are too distracted to eat. Do not worry unduly if your puppy seems disinterested in his food for the first day or so. Give him 10 minutes to eat what he wants and then remove the leftovers and start afresh at the next meal. Obviously if you have any concerns about your puppy in the first few days, seek advice from your vet.

If your Yorkie seems to lose interest in his food, try feeding him in his crate where he can eat in peace and will not be so distracted. It is also advisable to work at your Yorkshire Terrier's food manners so he never feels threatened when he is eating and does not become protective of his food bowl. You can do this by giving him half his ration, and then dropping food around his bowl. This will stop him guarding his bowl and, at the same time, he will see your

presence in a positive light. You can also call him away from the bowl and reward him with some food – maybe something extra special – which he can take from your hand.

Start doing this as soon as your puppy arrives in his new home, and continue working on it throughout his life.

The first night

Your puppy will have spent the first weeks of his life with his mother or curled up with his siblings. He is then taken from everything he knows as familiar, lavished with attention by his new family – and then comes bed time when he is left all alone. It is little wonder that he feels abandoned.

The best plan is to establish a night-time routine, and then stick to it so that your puppy knows what is expected of him. Take your puppy into the garden to relieve himself, and then settle him in his crate. Some people leave a low light on for the puppy at night for the first week, others have tried a radio as company or a ticking clock. A covered hot-water bottle, filled with warm water, can also be a comfort. Like people, puppies are all individuals and what works for one, does not necessarily work for another, so it is a matter of trial and error.

Be very positive when you leave your puppy on his own. Do not linger, or keep returning; this will make the situation more difficult. It is inevitable that he will protest to begin with, but if you stick to your routine, he will accept that he gets left at night – but you always return in the morning.

Rescued dogs

Settling an older, rescued dog in the home is very similar to a puppy in as much as you will need to make the same preparations regarding his homecoming. As with a puppy, an older dog will need you to be consistent, so start as you mean to go on.

There is often an initial honeymoon period when you bring a rescued dog home, where he will be on his best behaviour for the first few weeks. It is after these first weeks that the true nature of the dog will show, so be prepared for subtle changes in his behaviour.

It may be advisable to register with a reputable training club, so you can seek advice on any training or behavioural issues at an early stage.

Above all, remember that a rescued dog ceases to be a rescued dog the moment he enters his forever home and should be treated like any other family pet.

House
training

This is an aspect of training that first-time dog owners dread, but if you start as you mean to go on, it will not be long before your Yorkshire Terrier understands what is required.

The key to successful house training is vigilance and consistency. If you establish a routine, and you stick to it, your puppy will understand what is required. Equally, you must be there to supervise him at all times – except when he is safely tucked up in his crate. It is when a puppy is left to wander from room to room that accidents are most likely to happen.

As discussed earlier, you will have allocated a toileting area in your garden when preparing for your puppy's homecoming. You need to take your puppy to this area every time he needs to relieve himself so he builds up an association and knows why you have brought him out to the garden.

Establish a routine and make sure you take your puppy out at the following times:

- First thing in the morning.

- After mealtimes

- On waking from a sleep.

- Following a play session.

- Last thing at night.

A puppy should be taken out to relieve himself every two hours as an absolute minimum. If you can manage an hourly trip out, so much the better. The more often your puppy gets it 'right', the quicker he will learn to be clean in the house. It helps if you use a verbal cue, such as "busy", when your pup is performing and, in time, this will trigger the desired response.

Do not be tempted to put your puppy out on the doorstep in the hope that he will toilet on his own. Most pups simply sit there, waiting to get back inside the house! No matter how bad the weather is, accompany your puppy and give him lots of praise when he performs correctly.

Do not rush back inside as soon as he has finished, your puppy might start to delay in the hope of prolonging his time outside with you. Praise him, have a quick game – and then you can both return indoors.

When accidents happen

No matter how vigilant you are, there are bound to be accidents. If you witness the accident, take your puppy outside immediately, and give him lots of praise if he finishes his business out there.

If you are not there when he has an accident, do not scold him when you discover what has happened. He will not remember what he has done and will not understand why you are cross with him. Simply clean it up and resolve to be more vigilant next time.

Make sure you use a deodoriser, available in pet stores, when you clean up, otherwise your pup will be drawn to the smell and may be tempted to use the same spot again.

Choosing
a diet

There are so many different types of dog food on sale – all claiming to be the best – so how do you know what is likely to suit your Yorkshire Terrier? A well-balanced diet is key to your Yorkie's health and wellbeing, so you need to do your homework in order to make the right decision.

When choosing a diet, there are basically three categories to choose from:

Complete

This is probably the most popular diet as it is easy to feed and is specially formulated with all the nutrients your dog needs. This means that you should not add any supplements or you may upset the nutritional balance.

Most complete diets come in different life stages - puppy, adult maintenance and senior, so this means that your Yorkshire Terrier is getting what he needs when he is growing, during adulthood, and as he becomes older. You can even get prescription diets for dogs with particular health issues.

Generally, an adult maintenance diet should contain 21-24 per cent protein and 10-14 per cent fat. Protein levels should be higher in puppy diets, and reduced in veteran diets.

Canned/pouches

This type of food, known as wet food, is usually fed with hard biscuit, and most Yorkies find it very appetizing. However, the ingredients – and the nutritional value – do vary significantly between the different brands so you will need to check the label. The more natural wet foods contain rice rather than other cereals containing gluten, so select this type to avoid allergic reactions.

Bear in mind that wet foods, as their name indicates, often have a high moisture content, so you need to be sure your Yorkie is getting all the nutrition he needs.

Homemade

There are some owners who like to prepare meals especially for their dogs – and it is probably much appreciated. The danger is that although the food is tasty, and your Yorkshire Terrier may enjoy the variety, you cannot be sure that it has the correct nutritional balance. If this is a route you want to go down, you will need to find out the exact ratio of fats, carbohydrates, proteins, minerals and vitamins that are needed, which is quite an undertaking. The Barf (Biologically Appropriate Raw Food) diet is another, more natural approach to feeding. Dogs are fed a diet mimicking what they would have eaten in the wild, consisting of raw meat, bone, muscle, fat, and vegetable matter. You may think that this is too much for a Toy Dog to cope with, but this is not the case. Yorkies, like many of the toy breeds, do not have the best teeth, and this diet can make a significant difference to dental health.

There are now a number of companies that specialise in producing the Barf diet in frozen form, which will make your job a lot easier.

Feeding regime

When your puppy arrives in his new home he will need four meals, evenly spaced throughout the day. You may decide to keep to the diet recommended by your puppy's breeder, and if your pup is thriving there is no need to change. However, if your puppy is not doing well on the food, or you have problems with supply, you will need to make a change.

When switching diets, it is very important to do it on a gradual basis, changing over from one food to the next, a little at a time, and spreading the transition over a week to 10 days.

This will avoid the risk of digestive upset. When your puppy is around 12 weeks, you can cut out one of his meals; he may well have started to leave some of his food indicating he is ready to do this. By six months, he can move on to two meals a day – a regime that will suit him for the rest of his life.

Do not allow your puppy to dictate when it comes to mealtimes.

Faddy feeders

If your Yorkshire Terrier is reluctant to eat, especially during the settling in period, it is tempting to try to tempt his appetite.

One look from those dark eyes is enough to melt your heart, stirring you to greater efforts to find a food that he will really like.

At first you may add some gravy, then you may try some chicken... The clever Yorkie will quickly realize that if he holds out, tastier treats will follow.

This is a bad game to play as not only will you run out of tempting delicacies, you will also be losing your Yorkie's respect.

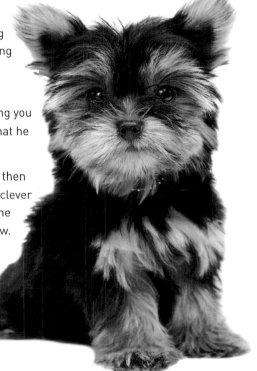

If your dog is turning up his nose at mealtimes, give him 10 minutes to eat what he wants, and then take up his bowl and give him fresh food at his next mealtime.

Do not feed him treats in between meals. If you continue this regime for a couple of days, your Yorkie will realize that there is no percentage in holding out for better food as it never materializes.

In most cases, this is just a 'trying it on' phase, and if you cope with commonsense, you will soon return to the status quo and your Yorkie will be content with his normal rations.

If, however, your dog refuses all food for more than 24 hours you need to observe his behaviour to see if there are any signs of ill health, which may involve the need for a veterinary check up.

Bones and chews

Puppies love to chew, and many adults also enjoy gnawing on a bone. A raw marrow bone is ideal, but make sure it is always given under supervision.

Rawhide chews are best avoided; even a dog as small as a Yorkie can bite off a chunk and swallow it, with the danger of it then causing a blockage.

Ideal weight

In order to help to keep your Yorkshire Terrier in good health it is necessary to monitor his weight. Obesity is a major problem among the canine population, and a dog that is fed too much, often coupled with insufficient exercise, is likely to pile on the pounds.

A dog that is carrying too much weight is vulnerable to many health issues; he has a poorer quality of life as he cannot exercise properly, and he will almost certainly have a reduced life expectancy.

When judging your Yorkshire Terrier's condition, look at him from above, and make sure you can see a definite 'waist'.

You should be able to feel his ribs, but not see them. It is easy for a Yorkie's coat to mask his weight, even when the coat is clipped, so it is a good idea to get into the habit of visiting your veterinary surgery on a monthly basis so that you can weigh your dog.

You can keep a record of his weight so you can make adjustments if necessary. If you are concerned that your Yorkie is putting on too much weight, or equally if you think he is underweight, consult your vet, who will help you to plan a suitable diet.

Caring for your Yorkie

The big question with a Yorkshire Terrier is whether you are going to keep him in full coat or opt for a pet trim. This will have a huge impact on your workload.

The Yorkshire Terrier has fine, silky hair that just keeps on growing! This is a feature of the breed, and the sight of a Yorkie in full coat is indeed spectacular. However, it is unlikely that you will opt for this unless you are going to show your dog. But even if you decide on a pet trim, the Yorkie's coat needs regular grooming.

For this reason, it is important to start as you mean to go on and accustom your puppy to being groomed. In this way, he will accept the attention without fuss, and may even enjoy it.

A grooming session also gives you the opportunity

to check your dog and to discover any minor problems, such as sore places, or any abnormalities, such as lumps and bumps which may need to be investigated. Remember, if you spot a problem early on, you increase the chance of an early diagnosis and successful treatment.

The first step is to get your puppy used to being handled. Initially, he will wriggle and attempt to mouth you, but just ignore his protests. Hold him steady for a few moments, and reward him when he is still. A puppy needs to learn that it is OK to be touched all over; if you fail to do this, he may try to warn you off by growling, which could develop into more problematic behaviour.

Start by handling your puppy all over, stroking him from his head to his tail. Lift up each paw in turn, and reward him with a treat when he co-operates. Then roll him over on to his back and tickle his tummy; this is a very vulnerable position for a dog to adopt, so do not force the issue. Be firm but gentle, and give your Yorkie lots of praise when he does as you ask.

When you start grooming, place your puppy on a rubber mat to prevent him from slipping. You will need a steel comb with half coarse teeth and half fine teeth, and a pure bristle brush. Start with the

When your puppy has stood still for a short period, reward him.

Hold him steady and be gentle as you check his ears.

Pick up each paw in turn so you can examine the pads and nails.

face and gently comb all over, paying particular attention to the chest and undercarriage. Keep a water spray bottle at your side,and use it if you come across a knot in the coat. Moistening the hair will help you to tease out the knot with the minimum of discomfort.

When you have finished combing, repeat the whole process, this time brushing through the coat. By this stage it should be tangle free so you should be able to proceed quite easily.

The more you brush, the more the coat will shine! Check your puppy's rear end and clean if necessary. This routine should be started in puppyhood and continued throughout your Yorkie's life. Most owners find that grooming two or three times a week keeps the coat in good order.

Pet trim

There are lots of different trimming styles – the choice is yours! You can take your dog to a grooming parlour for a professional clip, or you can do it yourself if you are handy with a pair of scissors.

Some owners prefer a short coat, others prefer to allow some length, keeping sufficient head furnishing for a topknot. If you do not wrap the coat (see below), it will not grow to floor length, and

regular trimming will ensure it does not become too difficult to deal with.

Bathing

Unlike the majority of breeds, the Yorkshire Terrier does not have natural oils in his coat and therefore he will need regular bathing. For a pet Yorkie, consider bathing every couple of weeks using a high-quality shampoo and conditioner, making sure you rinse throughly before drying the coat.

Bathing a full-coated Yorkie is a major undertaking as the coat will knot very easily. Take extra care when drying, squeezing the excess moisture from the coat rather than rubbing with a towel. You will then need to use a hair-dryer, brushing the coat constantly to make sure it does not become wavy.

Wrapping the coat

If you plan to keep your Yorkshire Terrier in full coat, you will need to keep it in wrappers to prevent damaging it. This is a process which involves wrapping sections of hair in tissue paper, and then folding them into small envelopes, secured with rubber bands.

A Yorkie's coat grows as he matures, and to begin with a puppy will only need a couple of wrappers on his back legs, which act as mini boots. As the

Facing page: The Yorkie's long hair has to be protected from everyday wear and tear.

hair grows he will also need a wrap for his head furnishings.

When your Yorkie is around 12 months of age, you will need to wrap his entire coat. To do this, apply almond oil to the coat, using a brush, which will make the coat easier to handle.

Everyone has their own method of wrapping or crackering the coat, but most start with the head furnishings and progress along the length of the body. When the coat is fully wrapped, you can put your Yorkie in a loose fitting coat, which will keep all the wrappers in place and allow him the freedom to run and play.

Show dogs are kept in wrappers full time, although they are removed and the coat is bathed regularly. The only time the coat is revealed in its full glory is on show days.

The coat is brushed to perfection to bring out its brilliant gleam, and the picture is completed with a traditional red ribbon to tie the topknot.

Routine care

In addition to grooming, you will need to carry out some routine care.

Eyes

Check the eyes for signs of soreness or discharge.
If there is debris around the eye, you can use a piece
of cotton wool (cotton) – a separate piece for each
eye – for cleaning. However, if there is discharge
from the eye, you should book a visit to the vet who
can examine the eyes and prescribe the appropriate
treatment.

Ears

Checking ears is essential with a Yorkshire Terrier
as hair tends to grow inside the ear. This needs to be
plucked out otherwise it can become dirty which can
then be a source of infection. Apply a little canker
powder inside the ear, and this will make it easier
for you to grip the hair with finger and thumb.

If the ear is dirty, you can clean it using damp cotton-
wool (cotton). Be careful not to probe into the ear
canal or you could do more harm than good. If your
dog's ears appear to be particularly dirty and foul-
smelling, consult your vet who will prescribe the
appropriate treatment.

Teeth

Dental disease is increasing among dogs so teeth
cleaning should be seen as an essential part of your
care regime, and this is particularly the case with Toy

Dogs, which are prone to dental problems. Bear in mind, the build up of tartar on the teeth can result in tooth decay, gum infection and bad breath, and if it is allowed to accumulate, you may have no option but to get the teeth cleaned under anaesthetic.

When your Yorkshire Terrier is still a puppy, accustom him to teeth cleaning so it becomes a matter of routine. Dog toothpaste comes in a variety of meaty flavours, which your Yorkie will like, so you can start by putting toothpaste on your finger and gently rubbing his teeth. You can then progress to using a finger brush or a toothbrush, whichever you find most convenient.

Remember to reward your Yorkie when he co-operates and then he will positively look forward to his teeth-cleaning sessions.

Nails

Nail trimming is a task dreaded by many owners – and many dogs – but, again, if you start early on, your Yorkshire Terrier will get used to the task you have to perform and will not fight against it.

The Yorkshire Terrier should have black nails (as opposed to white) which means you cannot see the quick, which is the vein that runs through the nail. This makes nail trimming more difficult as

Facing page: Accustom your Yorkie to nail trimming from an early age.

you need to avoid cutting into the quick. If you do this inadvertently, it is not disastrous, but it will cause the nail to bleed profusely. This will be uncomfortable for your Yorkie, and he will remember it next time you attempt to trim his nails. The best policy is to trim little and often so the nails don't grow too long, and you do not risk cutting too much and catching the quick.

If you are worried about trimming your Yorkie's nails, go to your vet so you can see it done properly. If you are still concerned, you can always use the services of a professional groomer.

Exercise

The Yorkshire Terrier thrives on having a busy, interesting life, and although he does not require extensive exercise, he does need variety and stimulation. Every dog, regardless of size, needs to use his body in order to stay fit and healthy. In addition, he will benefit hugely if he is given the opportunity to explore new places and investigate different smells.

For the first couple of months after arriving in his new home, a Yorkie puppy will be content with playing in the garden, with short outings for socialisation purposes. This can be increased gradually, with limited lead-walking, which

Facing page: Your Yorkie will relish the opportunity to run and burn off surplus energy.

youngsters find very tiring. Your puppy should also have the opportunity to let off steam, free running for 10 minutes or so.

When your Yorkie is fully grown, you can adopt an exercise regime to suit your own lifestyle. A Yorkie will make do with limited exercise, provided he has an active, interesting home life, or he will build up the stamina to go on longer expeditions. The Yorkie is a great hunter, dating back to his rat-catching ancestry, and you will be highly entertained by his antics – even if it takes him a while to come back your side! For information on recall training, see page 138.

Playing games

This is a great way of providing physical exercise and mental stimulation. The Yorkie is playful and inquisitive, and he will love interacting with you and earning rewards. The more you play with him, the more he will enjoy it and the two of you can become increasingly inventive with games of search and retrieve, and maybe some trick training thrown in for good measure.

If your Yorkie is a bit of a foodie, there is a game you can play which will use his mental energies and make use of his sense of smell. Once in a while, do not give your Yorkie his food in a bowl but scatter it over a small area in the garden. Let your Yorkie see what you are doing, and then encourage him to "find" his dinner. There are few dogs who can resist this, and they will positively relish the task of seeking out their food.

The older Yorkshire Terrier

We are fortunate that Yorkshire Terriers enjoy a good life expectancy. With luck, most dogs will reach their early teens, and some may exceed this. However, it is inevitable that a Yorkie will slow up as he gets older so you need to keep a close check to monitor this change.

The older Yorkie may sleep more and he may be reluctant to go for longer walks. He may show signs of stiffness when he gets up from his bed, but these generally ease when he starts moving.

Some older Yorkshire Terriers may have impaired vision, and some may become a little deaf, but as long as their senses do not deteriorate dramatically, this is something older dogs learn to live with.

If you treat your older dog with kindness and consideration, he will enjoy his later years and suffer the minimum of discomfort. It is advisable to switch him over to a senior diet, which is more suited to his needs, and you may need to adjust the quantity, as he will not be burning up the calories as he did when he was younger and more energetic.

Make sure his sleeping quarters are warm and free from draughts, and if he gets wet, make sure you dry him thoroughly.

Most important of all, be guided by your Yorkie. He will have good days when he feels up to going for a walk, and other days when he would prefer to potter in the garden.

If you have a younger dog at home, this may stimulate your Yorkie to take more of an interest in what is going on, but make sure he is not pestered, as he needs to rest undisturbed when he is tired.

Letting go

Inevitably there comes a time when your Yorkie is not enjoying a good quality of life, and you need to make the painful decision to let him go. We would all wish that our dogs died, painlessly, in their sleep but, unfortunately, this is rarely the case.

However, we can allow our dogs to die with dignity, and to suffer as a little as possible, and this should be our way of saying thank you for the wonderful companionship they have given us.

When you feel the time is drawing close, talk to your vet, who will be able to make an objective assessment of your Yorkie's condition and will help you to make the right decision.

This is the hardest thing you will ever have to do as a dog owner, and it is only natural to grieve for your beloved Yorkie.

But eventually, you will be able to look back on the happy memories of times spent together, and this will bring much comfort.

You may, in time, feel that your life is not complete without a Yorkshire Terrier, and you will feel ready to welcome a new puppy into your home.

Social skills

To live in the modern world, without fear and anxieties, a Yorkshire Terrier needs to receive an education in social skills so that he learns to cope calmly and confidently in a wide variety of situations. This is a little dog facing a big world and he needs to have both the confidence and the self control to become a model canine citizen.

Early learning

The breeder will have begun a programme of socialisation by getting the puppies used to all the sights and sounds of a busy household. You need to continue this when your pup arrives in his new home, making sure he is not worried by household equipment, such as the vacuum cleaner or the washing machine, and that he gets used to unexpected noises from the radio and television.

To begin with, your puppy needs to get used to all the members of his new family, but then you should give him the opportunity to meet friends and other people that come to the house. If you do not have children of your own, make sure your puppy has the chance to meet and play with other people's children – making sure interactions are always supervised – so he learns that humans come in small sizes, too.

Home alone

The Yorkie adores his family, and within weeks of arriving in his new home, he will form a strong bond with his human pack. This is brilliant, but be careful. A Yorkie also needs to learn to cope on his own otherwise he will develop separation anxiety. This happens when a dog panics if he is left on his own because he fears he is being abandoned.

Instead of settling quietly until his family return, the anxious dog will become increasingly distressed. He may bark or whine constantly, he may become destructive, and he may even soil his sleeping quarters.

This should never be seen as a compliment – a sign of how much your Yorkie loves you. It is simply a lack of training which causes your dog acute distress. Right from the start, you need to accustom your dog to short periods on his own.

Ideally, settle him in his crate with a boredom busting toy, such as a kong, filled with food, and leave him alone for a short period. When you return, do not make a big fuss of him. You could even wait a few minutes before you go to his crate, just to let him know that you are back, but it's no big deal.

Gradually increase the amount of time you leave your Yorkie, so that you are confident that he will settle happily for a couple of hours.

Keep leaving rituals to a minimum so your Yorkie does not start getting worried as he anticipates your departure, and be relaxed and calm when you return. In this way your Yorkie will learn that arrivals and departures are part of daily life and are not the cause of anxiety.

The outside world

When your puppy has completed his vaccinations, he is ready to venture into the outside world. As a breed, the Yorkshire Terrier is generally confident but there is a lot for a youngster to take on board, so do not swamp him with too many new experiences when you first set out.

Obviously you need to work at lead-training (see page 136) before you set out on your first expedition. There will be plenty of distractions to cope with, so you do not want additional problems of coping with a dog that is pulling or lagging on the lead.

So, hopefully, you can set off with your Yorkie walking by your side on a loose lead. He may need additional encouragement when you venture further afield, so arm yourself with some extra special treats, which will give him a good reason to focus on you when required!

Start socialising your puppy in a quiet area with light traffic, and only progress to a busier place when he is ready.

There is so much to see and hear – people (maybe carrying bags or umbrellas), pushchairs, bicycles, cars, lorries, machinery – so give your puppy a chance to take it all in.

Lessons learnt in puppyhood will stand your Yorkie in good stead throughout his life.

If he does appear worried, do not fall into the trap of sympathising with him, or worse still, picking him up. This will only teach your pup that he had a good reason to be worried and, with luck, you will 'rescue' him if he feels scared.

Instead, give a little space so he does not have to confront whatever he is frightened of, and distract him with a few treats. Then ask him to walk past, using an encouraging tone of voice, never forcing him by yanking on the lead. Reward him for any forward movement, and your puppy will soon learn that he can trust you, and there is nothing to fear.

Dog-to-dog meetings

Your pup also needs to continue his education in canine manners, started by his mother and by his littermates, as he needs to be able to greet all dogs calmly, giving the signals that say he is friendly.

The Yorkie is small in size – but not in his own mind. He does not see the need to be submissive with other dogs – he's a fiesty terrier and proud of it. As a result, a Yorkie can get himself into trouble, and situations can escalate out of control. You need to treat your little Yorkie just as you would any other dog and ensure that he develops good meeting and greeting skills with other dogs.

Try the following:

- Find a friend who has a dog with a bombproof temperament and visit their house. Allow the two dogs to play in the garden for 10 minutes or so. Do not prolong the game, as you do not want your youngster to become over-excited, or overwhelmed.

- Once the two dogs have had a few play-dates at home, go for a walk and allow them to exercise together off lead. They will interact with each other, but their focus will shift periodically, as they will be distracted by other sights and smells.

- Extend your Yorkie's circle of acquaintance by finding other friends who have dogs of sound temperament, ideally ranging over a number of different breeds. The more your Yorkie practises meeting and greeting, the better he will become at reading body language and assessing other dogs' intentions.

Training classes

A training class will give your Yorkshire Terrier the opportunity to work alongside other dogs in a controlled situation, and he will also learn to focus on you in a different, distracting environment. Both these lessons will be vital as your dog matures. However, the training class needs to be of the highest calibre or you risk doing more harm than good. Before you go along with your puppy, attend a class as an observer to make sure you are happy with what goes on.

Find out the following:

- How much training experience do the instructors have?

- Are the classes divided into appropriate age categories?

- Do they use positive, reward-based training methods?

- Do any of the instructors have experience with Yorkshire Terriers?

If the training class is well run, it is certainly worth attending. Both you and your Yorkie will learn useful training exercises.

It will also increase his social skills, and you will have the chance to talk to lots of like-minded dog enthusiasts.

Training Guidelines

Like all puppies, a young Yorkshire Terrier will soak up new experiences like a sponge, so training should start from the time your pup arrives in his new home.

You will be keen to get started, but in your rush to get training underway, do not neglect the fundamentals that could make the difference between success and failure.

You need to get into the mindset of a Yorkshire Terrier, working out what makes him tick and, equally, what makes him switch off.

Decide on your priorities for training, set realistic targets, and then think of ways of making your training as positive, and as fun, as possible.

When you start training, try to observe the following guidelines:

- Choose an area that is free from distractions so your puppy will focus on you. You can progress to a more challenging environment as your pup progresses.

- Do not train your puppy just after he has eaten or when you have returned from exercise. He will either be too full, or too tired, to concentrate.

- Do not train if you are in a bad mood, or if you are short of time – these sessions always end in disaster!

- Providing a worthwhile reward is an essential tool in training. You will probably get the best results if you use some extra special food treats, such as cheese or cooked liver. Although some Yorkies get very focused on toys, and will see a game with a favourite toy as a top reward.

- If you decide to use a toy, make sure it is only brought out for training sessions, so that it accrues added value.

- Keep your verbal cues simple, and always use the same one for each exercise. For example, when you ask your puppy to go into the Down position, the cue is "Down", not "Lie Down" or Get Down". Remember your Yorkie does not speak English; he associates the sound of the word with the action.

- If your dog is finding an exercise difficult, break it down into small steps so it is easier to understand.

- Do not make your training sessions boring and repetitious. The Yorkie is quick witted and prefers to work at a fast pace. If training is dull, he will lose focus and go off to find something more interesting to do!

- Do not train for too long, particularly with a young puppy that has a very short attention span, and always end training sessions on a positive note. This does not necessarily mean getting an exercise right. If your pup is tired and making mistakes, ask him to do a simple exercise so you have the opportunity to praise and reward him. You may well find that he benefits from having a break and will make better progress next time you try.

Remember that if your Yorkshire Terrier is rewarded for a behaviour, he is likely to repeat it – so make sure you are 100 per cent consistent and always reward the 'right' behaviour.

|First lessons

The Yorkshire Terrier is a clever dog and is quick to learn. He will enjoy training sessions as he likes to use his brain, but make sure you keep them rewarding so your Yorkie is motivated to co-operate and will enjoy spending quality time with you.

Wearing a collar

You may, or may not, want your Yorkshire Terrier to wear a collar all the time – this may depend on whether you are keeping him in full coat or not. But when he goes out in public places he will need to be on a lead, and so he should be used to the feel of a collar around his neck. The best plan is to accustom your pup to wearing a soft collar for a few minutes at a time until he gets used to it.

Fit the collar so that you can get at least two fingers between the collar and his neck. Then have a game to distract his attention.

This will work for a few moments; then he will stop,

put his back leg up behind his neck and scratch away at the peculiar itchy thing round his neck, which feels so odd.Bend down, rotate the collar, pat him on the head and distract him by playing with a toy or giving him a treat. Once he has worn the collar for a few minutes each day, he will soon ignore it and become used to it.

Remember, never leave the collar on the puppy unsupervised, especially when he is outside in the garden, or when he is in his crate, as it is could get snagged, causing serious injury.

Walking on the lead

This is a simple exercise, but the Yorkie can be a little stubborn, so it is a good idea to master the basics at home before venturing into the outside world where there is so much to distract him.

Once your puppy is used to the collar, take him outside into your secure garden where there are no distractions.Attach the lead and, to begin with, allow him to wander with the lead trailing, making sure it does not become snagged. Then pick up the lead and follow the pup where he wants to go; he needs to get used to the sensation of being attached to you.

The next stage is to get your Yorkie to follow you, and for this you will need some treats. To give yourself the best chance of success, make sure the treats are high value – cheese, sausage or cooked liver – so your Yorkie is motivated to work with you.

Show him you have a treat in your hand, and then encourage him to follow you. Walk a few paces, and if he is walking with you, stop and reward him. If he puts on the brakes, simply change direction and lure him with the treat.

Next introduce some changes of direction so your puppy is walking confidently alongside you. At this stage, introduce a verbal cue "Heel" when your puppy is in the correct position.

You can then graduate to walking your puppy outside the home – as long as he has completed his vaccination programme – starting in quiet areas and building up to busier environments. If you are struggling with your Yorkie on the lead, resist taking the easy option of picking him up.

This solves the immediate problem, but you are building up trouble ahead as your Yorkie will learn that jamming on the brakes offers an instant solution, and he does not need to do as you ask. Instead, arm yourself with lots of tasty treats, and give yourself plenty of time so you can reward your pup for co-operating, which means he is more likely to repeat the behaviour you want from him on future occasions.

Come when called

The Yorkshire Terrier is utterly devoted to his family, but there are times when he gets distracted. There are so many enticing smells out there, you can appreciate that an instant response to the recall may not always be his preferred option.

The key to successful recall training is to start early, and to teach your Yorkie to focus on you, regardless of distractions.

Hopefully, the breeder will have laid the foundations simply by calling the puppies to "Come" when it is dinnertime, or when they are moving from one place to another.

You can build on this when your puppy arrives in his new home, calling him to "Come" when he is in a confined space, such as the kitchen. This is a good place to build up a positive association with the verbal cue – particularly if you ask your puppy to "Come" to get his dinner!

The next stage is to transfer the lesson to the garden. Arm yourself with some treats, and wait until your puppy is distracted. Then call him, using a higher-pitched, excited tone of voice.

At this stage, a puppy wants to be with you, so capitalize on this and keep practising the verbal cue, rewarding your puppy with a treat and lots of praise when he comes to you.

Now you are ready to introduce some distractions. Try calling him when someone else is in the garden, or wait a few minutes until he is investigating a really interesting scent.

When he responds, make a really big fuss of him and give him some extra treats so he knows it is worth his while to come to you. If he is slow to come, run away a few steps and then call again, making yourself sound really exciting. Jump up and down, open your arms wide to welcome him; it doesn't matter how silly you look, he needs to see you as the most fun person in the world.

When you have a reliable recall in the garden, you can venture into the outside world.

Do not be too ambitious to begin with; try a recall in a quiet place with the minimum of distractions so you can be assured of success

Do not make the mistake of only asking your dog to come at the end of his allotted exercise period. What is the incentive in coming back to you if all you do is clip on his lead, marking the end of his free time?

Instead, call your dog at random times, giving him a treat and a stroke, and then letting him go free again. In this way, coming to you – and focusing on you – is always rewarding.

Stationary exercises

The Sit and Down are easy to teach,
and mastering these exercises
will be rewarding for both you
and your Yorkshire Terrier.

Sit

The best method is to lure your Yorkie into position, and for this you can use a treat or his food bowl.

Hold the reward (a treat or food bowl) above his head. As he looks up, he will lower his hindquarters and go into a sit.

Practise this a few times and when your puppy understands what you are asking, introduce the verbal cue, "Sit". When your Yorkie understands the exercise, he will respond to the verbal cue alone, and you will not need to reward him every time he sits. However, it is a good idea to give him a treat on a random basis when he co-operates to keep him guessing!

Down

This is an important lesson, and can be a lifesaver if an emergency arises and you need to bring your Yorkie to an instant halt.

You can start with your dog in a Sit or a Stand for this exercise. Stand or kneel in front of him and show him you have a treat in your hand. Hold the treat just in front of his nose and slowly lower it towards the ground, between his front legs.

As your Yorkie follows the treat he will go down on his front legs and, in a few moments, his

Facing Page: Build up the duration of the Down so your Yorkie stays in position until you release him.

hindquarters will follow. Close your hand over the treat so he doesn't cheat and get the treat before he is in the correct position. As soon as he is in the Down, give him the treat and lots of praise.

Keep practising, and when your Yorkie understands what you want, introduce the verbal cue "Down".

Control exercises

These exercises are not the most exciting, but they are especially important for a Yorkshire Terrier with a tendency to make up his own agenda. He needs to understand that he will be rewarded for making the right decision.

Wait

This exercise teaches your Yorkshire Terrier to "Wait" in position until you give the next command. It differs from the Stay exercise, where he must stay where you have left him for a more prolonged period. The most useful application of "Wait" is when you are getting your dog out of the car and you need him to stay in position until you clip on his lead.

Start with your puppy on the lead to give you a greater chance of success. Ask him to "Sit", then stand in front of him. Step back one pace, holding your hand, palm flat, facing him.

Wait a second and then come back to stand in front of him. You can then reward him and release him with a word, such as "OK".

Practise this a few times, waiting a little longer before you reward him, and then introduce the verbal cue "Wait".You can reinforce the lesson by using it in different situations, such as asking your Yorkie to "Wait" before you put his food bowl down.

Stay

You need to differentiate this exercise from the Wait by using a different hand signal and a different verbal cue. Start with your Yorkie in the Down, as he is most likely to be secure in this position. Stand by his side and then step forwards, with your hand held back, palm facing the dog.

Step back, release him, and then reward him. Practise until your Yorkie understands the exercise and then introduce the verbal cue "Stay".

Gradually increase the distance you can leave your puppy, and increase the challenge by walking around him – and even stepping over him – so that he learns he must "Stay" until you release him.

Leave

A response to this verbal cue means that your Yorkie will learn to give up a toy on request, and it follows that he will give up anything when he is asked, which is very useful if he has got hold of a forbidden object.

This is not simply a matter of obeying the verbal cue to "Leave"; it is establishing the status quo where you are the decision-maker and your Yorkie is ready to co-operate with you. This is particularly important with a Yorkie who can become possessive with favourite toys or places of high value, such as the sofa, or even your bed!

You can teach your Yorkie to co-operate without resorting to confrontation.

The "Leave" command can be taught quite easily when you are first playing with your puppy. As you gently, take a toy from his mouth, introduce the verbal cue, "Leave", and then praise him.

If he is reluctant, swap the toy for another toy or a treat. This will usually do the trick.

Do not try to pull the toy from his mouth if he refuses to give it up, as you will make the situation confrontational. Let the toy go 'dead' in your hand, and then swap it for a new toy, or a really high-value treat so this becomes the better option.

Remember to make a big fuss of your Yorkie when he does as you ask so that he learns that co-operation is always the best – and most rewarding – option.

This exercise can also be used if your Yorkie takes up a favourite position, such as on the sofa, and refuses to budge. Again the strategy is not to be confrontational but to offer him a better reward, such as a treat or a toy, and then call him to you.

As far as the Yorkie is concerned, he has not been forced to give up the thing he values, he has simply been offered something better

Try offering a substitute toy so you avoid conflict...

Opportunities for Yorkies

The Yorkshire Terrier has a brain and he will relish the chance to use it. The mistake most commonly made by owners of toys dogs is thinking that being small in size means training, particularly more advanced training, is not worth attempting. Nothing could be further from the truth. Give your Yorkie a chance to shine, and you will be amazed at what you can achieve together.

Good Citizen Scheme

The Kennel Club Good Citizen Scheme was introduced to promote responsible dog ownership, and to teach dogs basic good manners. In the US there is one test; in the UK there are four award levels: Puppy Foundation, Bronze, Silver and Gold.

Exercises within the scheme include:

- Walking on lead

- Road walking

- Control at door/gate.

- Food manners

- Recall

- Stay

- Send to bed

- Emergency stop

Agility

In Agility, the dog completes an obstacle course under the guidance of his owner. You need a good element of control, as the dog competes off the leash.

In competition, each dog is assessed on both time and accuracy. The dog that completes the course with the fewest faults, in the fastest time, wins the class. The obstacles include an A-frame, a dog-walk, weaving poles, a seesaw, tunnels, and jumps.

This may be too much for the smallest size of Yorkshire Terrier who are more likely to be destined for the show ring. A slightly bigger, sturdier Yorkie will be up to the task in hand, and will thoroughly enjoy using his quick wits to negotiate the equipment under the direction of his handler in the fastest possible time.

Rally O

This is loosely based on Obedience, and also has a few exercises borrowed from Agility when you get to the highest levels. Handler and dog must complete a course, in the designated order, which has a variety of different exercises that could number from 12 to 20. The course is timed and the team must complete within the time limit that is set, but there are no bonus marks for speed.

The great advantage of Rally O is that it is very relaxed, and anyone can compete; indeed, it has proved very popular for handlers with disabilities as they are able to work their dogs to a high standard and compete on equal terms.

Showing

The Yorkshire Terrier can be seen in his full glory in the show ring but there are number of factors that are integral to success in the ring.

Firstly you need a top quality Yorkie who adheres closely to the stipulations laid down in the Breed Standard. Secondly, you need to be skilled in grooming and show presentation, which is an art itself. Thirdly, you need a Yorkshire Terrier who is a natural show off and enjoys being in the ring. To prepare a Yorkshire Terrier for showing, he needs to be trained to stand on a box in show pose – this is the only breed to be shown in this way. He needs to be examined by a judge, and he must move correctly on a show lead, following a pattern dictated by the judge.

Heelwork to music

Also known as Canine Freestyle, this activity is becoming increasingly popular. Dog and handler perform a choreographed routine to music, allowing the dog to show off an array of tricks and moves, which delight the crowd. This discipline demands alot of training, but if rewards are on hand, and you keep it light-hearted, the Yorkie will prove to be a real crowd-pleaser!

|Health care

The Yorkshire Terrier is a healthy breed and, despite his small size, he is built without any other form of exaggeration in terms of his conformation. This means that he is an active little dog, and with a comprehensive programme of preventative care and good management he should suffer few significant health problems.

Vaccinations

Dogs are subject to a number of contagious diseases. In the old days, these were killers, and resulted in heartbreak for many owners. Vaccinations have been developed, and the occurrence of the major infectious diseases is now very rare. However, this will only remain the case if all pet owners follow a strict policy of vaccinating their dogs. There are vaccinations available for the following diseases:

Adenovirus: (Canine Adenovirus): This affects the liver; affected dogs have a classic 'blue eye'.

Distemper: A viral disease which causes chest and gastro-intestinal damage. The brain may also be affected, leading to fits and paralysis.

Parvovirus: Causes severe gastro enteritis, and most commonly affects puppies.

Leptospirosis: This bacterial disease is carried by rats and affects many mammals, including humans. It causes liver and kidney damage.

Rabies: A virus that affects the nervous system and is invariably fatal. The first signs are abnormal behaviour, when the infected dog may bite another animal or a person. Paralysis and death follow.

Vaccination is compulsory in most countries. In the UK, dogs travelling overseas must be vaccinated.

Kennel Cough: There are several strains of Kennel Cough, but they all result in a harsh, dry, cough. This disease is rarely fatal; in fact most dogs make a good recovery within a matter of weeks and show few signs of ill health while they are affected. However, Kennel Cough is highly infectious among dogs that live together so, for this reason, most boarding kennels will insist that your dog is protected by the vaccine, which is given as nose drops.

Lyme disease: This is a bacterial disease transmitted by ticks (see page 169). The first signs are limping, but the heart, kidneys and nervous system can also be affected. The ticks that transmit the disease occur in specific regions, such as the north-east states of the USA, some of the southern states, California and the upper Mississippi region. Lyme disease is still rare in the UK so vaccinations are not routinely offered.

Vaccination programme

In the USA, the American Animal Hospital Association advises vaccination for core diseases, which they list as: Distemper, Adenovirus, Parvovirus and Rabies. The requirement for vaccinating for non-core diseases – Leptospirosis, Lyme Disease and Kennel Cough – should be assessed depending on a dog's individual risk and his likely exposure to the disease.

In the UK, vaccinations are routinely given for Distemper, Adenovirus, Leptospirosis and Parvovirus.

In most cases, a puppy will start his vaccinations at around eight weeks of age, with the second part given a fortnight later. However, this does vary depending on the individual policy of veterinary

practices, and the incidence of disease in your area. You should also talk to your vet about whether to give annual booster vaccinations.

You need to plan a vaccination programme to protect your puppy from the major infectious diseases.

Parasites

No matter how well you look after your Yorkshire Terrier you will have to accept that parasites – internal and external – are ever present, and you need to take preventative action.

Internal parasites: As the name suggests, these parasites live inside your dog. Most will find a home in the digestive tract, but there is also a parasite that lives in the heart. If infestation is unchecked, a dog's health will be severely jeopardised, but routine preventative treatment is simple and effective.

External parasites: These parasites live on your dog's body – in his skin and fur, and sometimes in his ears.

Roundworm

This is found in the small intestine, and signs of infestation will be a poor coat, a potbelly, diarrhoea and lethargy. Pregnant mothers should be treated, but it is almost inevitable that parasites will be passed on to the puppies. For this reason, a breeder will start a worming programme, which you will need to continue. Ask your vet for advice on treatment, which you will need to continue throughout your dog's life.

Tapeworm

Infection occurs when fleas and lice are ingested; the adult worm lodges in the small intestine, releasing mobile segments (which contain eggs); these can be seen in a dog's faeces as small rice-like grains. The only other obvious sign of infestation is irritation of the anus. Again, routine preventative treatment is required throughout your Yorkie's life.

Heartworm

This parasite is transmitted by mosquitos, and so will only occur where these insects thrive. A warm environment is needed for the parasite to develop, so it is more likely to be present in areas with a warm, humid climate. However, it is found in all parts of the USA, although its prevalence does vary. At present, heartworm is rarely seen in the UK. Heartworm live in the right side of the heart. Larvae can grow up to 14 inches (35cm) in length. A dog with heartworm is at severe risk from heart failure, so preventative treatment, as advised by your vet, is essential. Dogs living in the USA should have regular blood tests to check for the presence of infection.

Lungworm

Lungworm, or *Angiostrongylus vasorum*, is a parasite that lives in the heart and major blood vessels supplying the lungs. It can cause many problems, such as breathing difficulties, blood-clotting problems, sickness and diarrhoea, seizures, and can even be fatal.

The parasite is carried by slugs and snails, and the dog becomes infected when ingesting these, often accidentally when rummaging through undergrowth. Lungworm is not common, but it is on the increase and a responsible owner should be aware of it. Fortunately, it is easily preventable and even affected dogs usually make a full recovery if treated early enough. Your vet will be able to advise you on the risks in your area and what form of treatment may be required.

Fleas

A dog may carry dog fleas, cat fleas, and even human fleas. The flea stays on the dog only long enough to have a blood meal and to breed, but its presence will result in itching and scratching.

If your dog has an allergy to fleas – which is usually a reaction to the flea's saliva – he will scratch himself until he is raw.Spot-on treatment, which should be administered on a routine basis, is easy to use and highly effective on all types of fleas. You can also treat your dog with a spray or with insecticidal shampoo. Bear in mind that the whole environment your dog lives in will need to be sprayed, and all other pets living in your home will also need to be treated.

How to detect fleas

You may suspect your dog has fleas, but how can you be sure? There are two methods to try.

Run a fine comb through your dog's coat, and see if you can detect the presence of fleas on the skin, or clinging to the comb. Alternatively, sit your dog on some white paper and rub his back. This will dislodge faeces from the fleas, which will be visible as small brown specks. To double check, shake the specks on to some damp cotton-wool (cotton). Flea faeces consist of the dried blood taken from the host, so if the specks turn a lighter shade of red, you know your dog has fleas.

Ticks

These are blood-sucking parasites, most frequently found in rural areas where sheep or deer are present. The main danger is their ability to pass Lyme disease to both dogs and humans. Lyme disease is prevalent in some areas of the USA (see page 163), although it is still rare in the UK. The treatment you give your dog for fleas generally works for ticks, but you should discuss the best product to use with your vet.

Ear mites

These parasites live in the outer ear canal. The signs of infestation are a brown, waxy discharge, and your dog will continually shake his head and scratch his ear. If you suspect your Yorkie has ear mites, visit your vet so medicated eardops can be prescribed.

Fur mites

These small, white parasites are visible to the naked eye and are often referred to as 'walking dandruff'. They cause a scurfy coat and mild itchiness, but they are zoonetic – transferable to humans – so prompt treatment with an insecticide prescribed by your vet is essential.

Harvest mites

These are picked up from the undergrowth, and can be seen as a bright orange patch on the webbing between the toes, although they can be found elsewhere on the body, such as on the earflaps. Treatment is effective with the appropriate insecticide.

Skin mites

There are two types of parasite that burrow into a dog's skin. *Demodex canis* is transferred from a mother to her pups while they are feeding. Treatment is with a topical preparation, and sometimes antibiotics are needed. The other skin mite is *Sarcoptes scabiei*. Both cause intense itching and hair loss.

They are highly contagious, so all dogs in a household will need to be treated, which involves repeated bathing with a medicated shampoo.

Common ailments

Like all living creatures, dogs can be affected by a variety of ailments. Most can be treated effectively after consulting with your vet, who will prescribe appropriate medication and will advise you on how to care for your dog's needs.

Here are some of the more common problems that could affect your Yorkshire Terrier with advice on how to deal with them.

Anal glands

These are two small sacs on either side of the anus, which produce a dark-brown secretion that dogs use when they mark their territory. The anal glands should empty every time a dog defecates but if they become blocked or impacted, a dog will experience increasing discomfort. He may nibble at his rear end,

or 'scoot' his bottom along the ground to relieve the irritation.

Treatment involves a trip to the vet, who will empty the glands manually. It is important to do this without delay, or infection may occur.

Dental problems

Routine teeth cleaning will do much to minimise gum infection and tooth decay, which affects many toy dogs, particularly as they get older. The Yorkshire Terrier is also prone to gingivitis – an inflammation of the gums - which is caused by poor dental hygiene.

If tartar accumulates to the extent that you cannot remove it by brushing, the vet will need to intervene. In a situation such as this, an anaesthetic will need to be administered so the tartar can be removed manually.

Diarrhoea

There are many reasons why a dog has diarrhoea, but most commonly it is the result of scavenging, a sudden change of diet, or an adverse reaction to a particular type of food.

If your dog is suffering from diarrhoea, the first step is to withdraw food for a day. It is important that he does not dehydrate, so make sure that fresh drinking water is available. However, drinking too much can increase the diarrhoea, which may be accompanied with vomiting, so limit how much he drinks at any one time.

After allowing the stomach to rest, feed a bland diet, such as white fish or chicken, with boiled rice for a few days. In most cases, your dog's motions will return to normal and you can resume normal feeding, although this should be done gradually.

However, if this fails to work and the diarrhoea persists for more than a few days, you should consult your vet. Your dog may have an infection, which needs to be treated with antibiotics, or the diarrhoea may indicate some other problem, which needs expert diagnosis.

Ear infections

The Yorkshire Terrier has small v-shaped ears which he carries erect. This allows air to circulate freely and so the Yorkie is not plagued with ear infections, which can affect breeds that have pendulous ears.

A healthy ear is clean with no sign of redness or inflammation, and no evidence of a waxy brown discharge or a foul odour. If you see your dog scratching his ear, shaking his head, or holding one ear at an odd angle, you will need to consult your vet.

The most likely causes are ear mites, an infection, or a foreign body, such as a grass seed, that may be trapped in the ear.

Depending on the cause, treatment is with medicated eardrops, possibly containing antibiotics. If a foreign body is suspected, the vet will need to carry our further investigations.

Eye problems

The Yorkshire Terrier has medium-sized eyes which should nor protrude. This is important as a breed such as the Pug that has prominent eyes will be more vulnerable to injury.

Healthy eyes are bright and sparkling with no sign of discharge.

If your Yorkie's eyes look red and sore, he is likely be suffering from conjunctivitis. This may, or may not be accompanied with a watery or a crusty discharge. Conjunctivitis can be caused by irritation to the eyeball, a bacterial or viral infection, the result of an injury, or it could be an adverse reaction to pollen.

You will need to consult your vet for a correct diagnosis, but in the case of an infection, treatment with medicated eye drops is effective. Conjunctivitis may also be the first sign of more serious inherited eye problems (see Entropion page 184).

In some instances, a dog may suffer from dry, itchy eye, which he may further injure through scratching. This condition, known as *keratoconjunctivitis sicca*, may be inherited.

Foreign bodies

In the home, puppies – and some older dogs – cannot resist chewing anything that looks interesting. The toys you choose for your dog should be suitably robust to withstand damage, but children's toys can be irresistible.

Some dogs will chew – and swallow – anything from socks, tights, and any other items from the laundry basket to golf balls and stones from the garden.

Obviously, these items are indigestible and could cause an obstruction in your dog's intestine, which is potentially lethal.

The signs to look for are vomiting, and a tucked up posture. The dog will often be restless and will look as though he is in pain.In this situation, you must get your dog to the vet without delay, as surgery will be needed to remove the obstruction.

Heatstroke

Many owners fail to appreciate that a dog may suffer from over-heating on warm days, and not just on days when the temperature soars. This is particularly the case if your dog undertaken rigorous exercise. If the weather is warm make sure your Yorkshire Terrier has access to shady areas, and wait for a cooler part of the day before going for a walk.

Be extra careful if you leave your Yorkie in the car, as the temperature can rise dramatically - even on a cloudy day. Heatstroke can happen very rapidly, and unless you are able to lower your dog's temperature, it can be fatal.

If your Yorkie appears to be suffering from heatstroke, lie him flat and work at lowering his temperature by spraying him with cool water and covering him with wet towels. As soon as he has made some recovery, take him to the vet where cold intravenous fluids can be administered.

Lameness/limping

There are a wide variety of reasons why a dog can go lame, from a simple muscle strain, to a fracture, ligament damage, or more complex problems with the joints, which may have an inherited basis (see page 186). If you are concerned about your dog, do not delay in seeking expert advice from your vet. As your Yorkie becomes more elderly, he may suffer from arthritis, which you will see as general stiffness, particularly when he gets up after resting.

It will help if you ensure his bed is in a warm draught-free location, and if your Yorkie gets wet after exercise, you must dry him thoroughly.

If your Yorkie seems to be in pain, consult your vet who will be able to help with pain relief medication.

Skin problems

Skin problems, usually seen as hair loss, soreness and itching, can have a variety of causes.

Fleas, and other external parasites can result in itching, and the skin can become very sore and inflamed if the dog has an allergic reaction. Preventative treatment is obviously essential, but if you suspect an allergic reaction, you may need to seek veterinary advice.

Food intolerance and environmental factors, such as dust mites or pollen, can also cause major skin problems. The problem here is finding the root cause, and this can only be done by a process of elimination, such as removing specific foods from the diet. Again, you will need help from your vet to deal with this issue.

Breed-specific conditions

Like all pedigree dogs, the Yorkshire Terrier does have a few breed-related disorders. If diagnosed with any of the diseases listed below, it is important to remember that they can affect offspring so breeding from affected dogs should be discouraged.

There are now recognised screening tests to enable breeders to check for affected individuals and hence reduce the prevalence of these diseases within the breed. DNA testing is also becoming more widely available, and as research into the different genetic diseases progresses, more DNA tests are being developed.

Eye conditions

The Yorkshire Terrier may be affected by three principle eye disorders:

Entopian

Entropion is the condition when a hair covered eyelid turns inwards, thus scratching the cornea or conjunctiva. If unattended, this can cause permanent damage and blindness. It is an extremely painful condition and is easily detected as the dog will suffer from excessive blinking and an abundantly watering eye. Surgery is reasonably straightforward and effective. Affected dogs should not be used in breeding programmes.

Hereditary cataracts

This is seen as a clouding of the lens, which progressively affects vision. It is generally seen in young or middle-aged dogs of up to four years old. There is a hereditary link so any dog with a history of this condition in their pedigree should be eliminated from breeding programmes.

Progressive Retinal Atrophy

This is a condition of the retina which affects both eyes. The first signs may be dilated pupils and an exaggerated luminosity from the eyes. Night blindness ensues and all vision is usually lost within a year of diagnosis. DNA tests are now available to determine whether dogs are PRA carriers.

Joint Disease

Legge-Perthes Disease

In this condition, the femoral head (ball) of the thighbone dies resulting in severe pain and lameness. Early diagnosis, treatment through pain relief, and resting the affected back leg in a sling may be effective, otherwise surgery will be required.

Patellar Luxation

This is where the kneecap slips out of position, causing the affected dog to bunny hop. This may be intermittent, with the patella quickly returning to its usual position or it may be more severe and require manual manipulation. Corrective surgery is available, but the results are variable.

Porto-systemic Shunt

A condition which occurs during development in the uterus and involves an abnormal blood vessel resulting in the liver being bypassed. This means that toxins usually processed by the liver enter the general circulation. The brain is most often affected, and there may be additional problems with the bladder and kidneys. The disease can be treated with medication and with corrective surgery if the abnormal blood vessel lies outside the liver.

Tracheal Collapse

The signs of this condition are a honking cough which is caused by the trachea or windpipe collapsing in on itself, thereby affecting the passage of air.

It is more likely to occur when the rate of respiration increases, so excitement, exercise, eating and drinking, and pulling on the lead will exacerbate the condition.

It is generally worse in obese dogs. The condition can be managed with medication and taking simple preventative measures such as avoiding obesity and walking an affected dog on a harness.

Summing up

It may give the pet owner cause for concern to find about health problems that may affect their dog.

But it is important to bear in mind that acquiring some basic knowledge is an asset, as it will allow you to spot signs of trouble at an early stage. Early diagnosis is very often the means to the most effective treatment.

Fortunately, the Yorkshire Terrier is generally a healthy and disease-free dog with his only visits to the vet being annual check-ups.

In most cases, owners can look forward to enjoying many happy years with this outstanding companion.

Useful addresses

Breed & Kennel Clubs
Please contact your Kennel Club to obtain contact information about breed clubs in your area.

UK
The Kennel Club (UK)
1 Clarges Street London, W1J 8AB
Telephone: 0870 606 6750
Fax: 0207 518 1058
Web: www.thekennelclub.org.uk

USA
American Kennel Club (AKC)
5580 Centerview Drive, Raleigh, NC 27606.
Telephone: 919 233 9767
Fax: 919 233 3627
Email: info@akc.org
Web: www.akc.org

United Kennel Club (UKC)
100 E Kilgore Rd, Kalamazoo,
MI 49002-5584, USA.
Tel: 269 343 9020
Fax: 269 343 7037
Web: www.ukcdogs.com/

Australia
Australian National Kennel Council (ANKC)
The Australian National Kennel Council is the administrative body for pure breed canine affairs in Australia. It does not, however, deal directly with dog exhibitors, breeders or judges. For information pertaining to breeders, clubs or shows, please contact the relevant State or Territory Body.

International
Fédération Cynologique Internationalé (FCI)
Place Albert 1er, 13, B-6530 Thuin, Belgium.
Tel: +32 71 59.12.38
Fax: +32 71 59.22.29
Web: www.fci.be

Training and behavior
UK
Association of Pet Dog Trainers
Telephone: 01285 810811
Web: www.apdt.co.uk

Canine Behaviour
Association of Pet Behaviour Counsellors
Telephone: 01386 751151
Web: www.apbc.org.uk

USA
Association of Pet Dog Trainers
Tel: 1 800 738 3647
Web: www.apdt.com

American College of Veterinary Behaviorists
Web: http://dacvb.org

American Veterinary Society of Animal Behavior
Web: www.avsabonline.org

Australia
APDT Australia Inc
Web: www.apdt.com.au

For details of regional behaviorists, contact the relevant State or Territory Controlling Body.

Activities

UK

Agility Club
www.agilityclub.co.uk/

British Flyball Association
Telephone: 01628 829623
Web: www.flyball.org.uk

USA

North American Dog Agility Council
Web: www.nadac.com/

North American Flyball Association, Inc.
Tel/Fax: 800 318 6312
Web: www.flyball.org

Australia

Agility Dog Association of Australia
Tel: 0423 138 914
Web: www.adaa.com.au

NADAC Australia
Web: www.nadacaustralia.com

Australian Flyball Association
Tel: 0407 337 939
Web: www.flyball.org.au

International

World Canine Freestyle Organisation
Tel: (718) 332-8336
Web: www.worldcaninefreestyle.org

Health

UK

British Small Animal Veterinary Association
Tel: 01452 726700
Web: www.bsava.com

Royal College of Veterinary Surgeons
Tel: 0207 222 2001
Web: www.rcvs.org.uk

www.dogbooksonline.co.uk/healthcare

Alternative Veterinary Medicine Centre
Tel: 01367 710324
Web: www.alternativevet.org

USA

American Veterinary Medical Association
Tel: 800 248 2862
Web: www.avma.org

American College of Veterinary Surgeons
Tel: 301 916 0200
Toll Free: 877 217 2287
Web: www.acvs.org

Canine Eye Registration Foundation
The Veterinary Medical DataBases
1717 Philo Rd, PO Box 3007,
Urbana, IL 61803-3007
Tel: 217-693-4800
Fax: 217-693-4801
Web: www.vmdb.org/cerf.html

Orthopaedic Foundation of Animals
2300 E Nifong Boulevard
Columbia, Missouri, 65201-3806
Tel: 573 442-0418
Fax: 573 875-5073
Web: www.offa.org

American Holistic Veterinary Medical
Association
Tel: 410 569 0795
Web: www.ahvma.org

Australia

Australian Small Animal Veterinary
Association
Tel: 02 9431 5090
Web: www.asava.com.au

Australian Veterinary Association
Tel: 02 9431 5000
Web: www.ava.com.au

Australian College Veterinary Scientists
Tel: 07 3423 2016
Web: acvsc.org.au

Australian Holistic Vets
Web: www.ahv.com.au